YOURSELF

For Your Father God Has Forgiven You!

JACQUELINE AKUA OWUSU, M.D.

Foreword by Bishop Joe Kwapong

Forgive Yourself, For Your Father God has Forgiven You

By Jacqueline Akua Owusu, M.D.

ISBN: 978-0-9840161-0-5
© Copyright 2011

For more Information: *www.livingfreenow.org*
PH: 478 484 7059

Dr. Jacqueline Akua Owusu (Dr. Jackie) can be contacted at *info@livingfreenow.org*

Printed in the United States of America

Cover design and layout: Tudor Maier *(www.tudormaier.com)*

Table of contents

DEDICATION

This book is dedicated to my husband Osei Bediako and our two sons, Matthew Bediako and Michael Bediako. Thank you for your constant support and love. For if you do not do what you do, I will not be able to do what I do. Many thanks again for believing in me and standing by me through the hardest of times.

Osei, when God laid it on my heart that you were my husband I was doubtful. Now I know that God does not make mistakes. I am so grateful that I was obedient in listening to Him concerning you. You have been one of the biggest blessings that God has bestowed upon me. May He continue to use you in ways that are unimaginable to you!

Matthew and Michael, thank you for letting me know how much I am loved even when I am not in your presence. I rededicate you back to our Father God. May He who created you and who knows your yesterday, today and tomorrow, place on your lives His perfect will and purpose for you both.

To God, thank you. I am so grateful to you. May you continue to use me and allow me to always be obedient to you for your Glory!

ACKNOWLEDGMENTS

Writing this book could not have been possible without those brave and transparent individuals who graciously shared their personal stories. By hearing their accounts, my life was forever transformed for the better. I trust yours will be too as you read on.

For the sake of privacy, their real names have been changed. They know who they are. My sincere gratitude and thanks goes out to them. I love you and pray that God continues to use you tremendously.

I am also grateful to Ms. Alice Owusu, my ever so supportive and sweet mother, my late father Stephen Kwame Owusu Sr., my grandmother Suzanne Tawiah, Nana Osei Bediako, my editors, Mr. & Mrs. James and Terilyn Burkhardt, Bishop & Mrs. Joe and Victoria Kwapong, Pastor Kwame Frimpong, Bishop Bob Hawkson, Bishop Eric Kwapong, Pastor Kofi Nyarko, Pastor Osei Kwabena Dadzie, Mr. & Mrs. Joseph and Veronica Addo, Mrs. Evelyn Afriyie, Mr. & Mrs. Twigg and Diane Minor, Dr. Habigail Cribe, Dr. Patricia Patterson, Dr. Olujoke Jones, Dr. Agnes Adu, Dr. Rachele de la Fuentes, Miss Akua Safo, Devon Owusu, Stephen Owusu Jr., the rest of my siblings, Mrs. Felicia Owusu, Miss Sharon Wooten, Ms. Emma Ivey, Mr. & Mrs. Angie and Harrison Payne, Pastor Cliff Hunter, Mr. Derrick Chatman, Mr. Bobby Sanders, and all the great men and women that I have had the privilege to work with at various hospitals who tirelessly give of themselves to provide the best healthcare for us all.

To my God, who is forever faithful and just, you know our hearts and I ask you to continue to use me as a vessel for your higher purpose and for your glory! Amen!

Foreword

BY BISHOP JOE KWAPONG

Alexander Pope, the third most frequently quoted writer in The Oxford Dictionary of Quotations, an 18th century English poet, best known for his satirical verse, is credited for the famous quote; "To err is human; To forgive, divine."

In one sense it may be true, because to forgive a person who wrongs you, takes a lot of "divine assistance," as the natural human reaction to every action, is an equal and opposite reaction. Especially when there is clear evidence that the perpetrator deliberately and repeatedly, has shown intent to hurt. Although this quote by Alexander Pope is widely accepted, it does not necessarily pass the biblical litmus test of true forgiveness.

On many occasions in the Holy Scriptures, Jesus spoke avidly about forgiveness, and its importance as it relates to our relationship with God, and our fellow humankind. *Matthew Chapter 18* for me, is one of several classic passages, where Jesus takes the time to offer a myriad of invaluable lessons. The chapter opens up with a discussion of who is the greatest in the kingdom of heaven, this is then followed by the parable of the lost sheep. This parable accentuates the fact that in the eyes of God, one considered a "little one" in the kingdom of God, has such colossal value that they warrant a shepherd leaving the ninety-nine sheep and going after the one that has rambled away.

In the next dialogue, Jesus began to teach, and to lay out instructions on how to deal with the complicated subject of offense, and the perpetrators who commit such hideous acts. Prompted by this discussion, Peter asks: *"Lord, how many times shall I forgive my brother or sister who sins against me? Up to seven times?"*

Old testament tradition, probably based on passages such as Amos 1:3, 6, & 9 and Job 33:29-30, seem to indicate that forgiveness was limited to three times. I can only assume that Peter, armed with this information, thought his willingness to forgive seven times was much more sufficient than the Jewish tradition. "Let's see what the master thinks of me now," I can imagine Peter thinking. Finally, a gesture that exceeds the righteousness of the Pharisees and teachers of the law!

To Peter's disappointment, Jesus was hardly impressed with his words. Instead, Jesus answered, *"I tell you, not seven times, but seventy-seven times." Other translations say* "seventy times seven."

I think the message and lesson from Jesus was clear, in spite of the version of translation! It strikes me as though Peter wanted to keep a count of the number of times to forgive, whereas Jesus was saying, as often as a person offends you, and comes to you asking for forgiveness, we ought to forgive! Forgiveness may be divine, but it is also a choice we can make! Whether we are Christians, Muslims, Atheist, or Agnostic, we have the capacity to forgive.

In *Proverbs 20:22*, the Bible declares; *"Do not say, I'll pay you back for this wrong! Wait for the LORD, and he will deliver you."* Again in *Colossians 3:13*, the Bible says; *"Bear with each other and forgive whatever grievances you may have against one another. Forgive as the Lord forgave you."* Another poignant passage that teaches the importance of forgiveness is found in *Matthew 6:9-15*. In that passage, Jesus teaches the model for prayer. After introducing worship, intercessory prayer, and prayer for our personal needs, he proceeds to talk about forgiveness. Jesus then says ingenuously in his closing arguments; *"For if you forgive men when they sin against you, your heavenly Father will also forgive you. But if you do not forgive men their sins, your Father will not forgive your sins."* Without mincing words, Jesus was saying "Your ability to receive forgiveness is predicated upon your capacity to forgive others."

The entire basis of God, so loving humankind, that He sacrificed His only son Jesus, is based upon His love and willingness to forgive our past, present, and future. God wants humankind reconciled back unto Him!

In her book *"FORGIVE YOURSELF", For Your Father God Has Forgiven You,* Dr. Jackie presents an in-depth exploration of the subject matter. Her stories are riveting, and as such, deal with real-life issues on how to practically deal with people on this subject of forgiveness. Dr Jackie is not inhibited to share her own past mistakes with you, and to meticulously walk you down the pathway that led to her own deliverance and restoration from her past. The emotional cleansing or catharsis, which took place deep in her soul that resulted in an outward expression, was a result of accepting forgiveness. First she had to accept the fact that through the blood of Jesus Christ, her past had been washed and forgiven. No longer was she the old person that dealt with the guilt of her past.

With the advancement of technology, and the proficiency of medical doctors such as Dr. Jackie Owusu, any patient with almost any medical condition that deals with internal medicine, can receive prognosis, diagnosis and treatment. However, who do you turn to for help, when you have been scarred by emotional wounds, and like a terminal disease, your life is wasting away gradually, undetected?

In reading this book, my recommendation is that you read it prayerfully, and not just browse through the pages so as to complete reading another book. Dr. Jackie is an uninhibited writer, who tells her story and others' in an unconventional way that is ingenuous. Her book will challenge you to take a second and third look at your life, while providing you with practical tools to help you make the choice to forgive yourself and others who may have hurt you from your past.

I hope that every person, Christian or non-Christian, invests time into the reading of this book, in order to benefit from the time- tested principles on the importance, and most of all, how to walk in forgiveness. Gerald Jampolsky, the child and adult psychiatrist, is quoted as saying: *"Forgiveness means letting go of the past."* To know this is the first step, but to be able to do this, is the practical step that will set you free! Forgiveness is to set a prisoner free, and to realize the prisoner was you.

Forgiveness is indeed a choice we have to make.
God Bless You!

Foreword written by:
Bishop Joe Kwapong
Presiding Pastor
River of Life Chapel
Lawrenceville, GA
(770) 769-7992
(678) 889-8622

Introduction

WHY DID I WRITE THIS BOOK?

"For God so loved the world that He gave His only begotten Son, that whoever believes in Him should not perish but have everlasting life."

(John 3:16)

Welcome friend, our meeting is not by chance. You could say it is by divine appointment. Does your life's circumstance make you feel completely lost with no way out? Or that no one truly understands you? Do you see yourself as all alone in this world without a shred of hope and utterly distraught? Have you ever had the horrible thought of ending it all rip into your mind?

The enemy of your soul will love to keep you in this bondage by relentlessly attacking your life and mind. However, please keep reading on because this book has real answers for you. A light will shine on those feelings and reveal your solution to be revived and enjoy a fulfilled life once again.

To be candid, God has allowed me to write this book specifically to help you see that everyone has skeletons and things that we are not proud of lurking in our lives. Some linger in the past. Others plague us now. We cannot allow these stumbling blocks to prevent us from receiving our blessings. Relax. You will not be judged for I am only sharing what God has laid on my heart to minister to you.

This book is written for all of us who have sinned and are unable to forgive ourselves. I am here to tell you that all sin is equal in God's eyes. If you have sinned (whatever it may be), and you have realized what a terrible mistake you've made then you need to ask God for forgiveness.

If you've already experienced conviction by the Holy Spirit and sought God's forgiveness but are still unable to forgive yourself then *pray some more and allow God to help you forgive yourself and heal.* Be assured that if you have prayed for forgiveness then God has indeed forgiven you. Keep on reading and soon you'll personally discover God's unending mercy.

The pathway to being forgiven begins with accepting the source of our forgiveness from the One who has the power to forgive.

The Bible says: *"Jesus is the way, the truth, and the life and no one comes to the Father except through Him." (John 14:6)*

Forgiveness and salvation from sin is provided for every human being, including you and me. God lovingly gave

Jesus Christ, His sinless son to die on Calvary's cross for all our sins. By believing with your faith in that work, God offers us the free gift of eternal life. Therefore, the first thing we have to do is accept His son Jesus Christ as our personal savior and trust in Him for the eternal forgiveness of our sins.

Friend, according to God's perfect plan for salvation, Jesus Christ's blood on the cross at His death washed away your sins and made you right with God. The Bible says that *"the wages of sin is death."* Jesus lived a sinless life then died to pay that debt for all mankind once and for all. That includes you and me. Jesus died to set us free forever from the effects of sin... and live every moment of your life on this earth as a "forgiven" person.

If God the faithful and just Father through Jesus Christ has forgiven all our sins then who are we not to also extend forgiveness both to ourselves and to others?

By accepting Jesus Christ as your Lord and personal Savior through having faith in His life, death and resurrection, you will become born again and begin a brand new life. It is much like a baby learning how to walk. Crawling at first then taking the first toddling steps. You can expect to stumble sometimes along the way but *never take your eyes off the prize* – that being a deep and richly intimate relationship with our Holy and Loving God "the Father." This progression in our Christian life moves us ever so closer to becoming more like Christ our Lord who lived the only sinless life and was one with the Father.

Also, pray to receive the fullness of the Holy Spirit. The Holy Spirit was sent after the resurrection of Jesus to be a comforter for you. His function is to reveal God's truth and word to you. Ask for the Holy Spirit to minister to you. Seek to hear, understand and obey God's voice in your life. As your spiritual walk with Jesus Christ progresses, you will have times where you are doubtful. Have a conversation with the Father in Jesus Name and let Him know your deepest fears and doubts. Have courage and take a leap of faith. See if your life is not radically transformed.

Chapter One

WHAT DOES THE BIBLE SAY ABOUT THE FORGIVENESS OF SINS?

The Bible says: "If we confess our sins, He is faithful and just to forgive us our sins and to cleanse us from all unrighteousness." (1 John 1:9)

Why does God forgive us of our sins?

There are many reasons why God forgives us. Here are four reasons why our sins are forgiven.

1. God forgives us of our sins because He is <u>compassionate.</u>

The Bible says in *(Micah 7:18-19), "Who is a God like you, who pardons sins and forgives the transgression of the remnant of his inheritance? You do not stay angry forever but delight to show mercy. You will again have compassion on us: you will tread ours sins underfoot and hurl all our iniquities into the depths of the sea."*

This verse shows how God has such a strong compassion for us that though we sin, He is able to forgive us.

2. God forgives us of our sins because of His _love._

In Psalm 51:1, David said, _"Have mercy upon me, O God, according to your unfailing love; according to your great compassion, blot out my transgression."_

This was David's humble prayer for forgiveness and cleansing of his sin after committing adultery with Bathsheba.

3. God forgives us of our sins because of His _grace._

The Bible says in Psalm 103:8-10, "The Lord is compassionate and gracious, slow to anger, abounding in love. He will not always accuse nor will he harbor His anger forever; He does not treat us as our sins deserve or repay us according to our iniquities."

4. God forgives us of our sins because of His _mercy._

In _Isaiah 55:7-8_, the Bible declares: _"Let the wicked forsake his way and the evil man his thoughts. Let him turn to the Lord, and He will have mercy on him, and to our God, for He will freely pardon. For My thoughts are not your thoughts, neither are your ways My ways, declares the Lord."_

How do we receive forgiveness of our sins from God?

Believe
Confess
Repent
Forgive Others

1. To receive forgiveness, as believers and non-believers, we must first _believe_ in Jesus Christ.

The Bible tells us that Jesus appeared to His disciples and opened their minds so they could understand the Scriptures.

In _Luke 24:46-47, Jesus said to His disciples, "This is what is written: The Christ will suffer and rise from the dead on the third day, and repentance and forgiveness of sins will be preached in His name to all nations."_

In _Acts 10:42-43,_ Peter states that, _"He, (Jesus), commanded us to preach to the people and to testify that He is the one whom God appointed as judge of the living and the dead. All the prophets testify about Him that everyone who believes in Him receives forgiveness of his sins through His name."_

2. We must _confess_ our sins to the Lord.

In _Psalm 32:5,_ David said, _"and then I acknowledged my sin to you and did not cover up my iniquity. I said, "I will confess my transgressions to the Lord and you forgave the guilt of my sin."_

3. We must _repent_ of our sins. As Peter was addressing a crowd at Pentecost, he made them aware that God made Jesus, whom they crucified, both Lord and Christ. When the crowd heard this, they asked what should they do and Peter said to them in _Acts 2:38, "Repent and be baptized, every one of you, in the name of Jesus Christ for the forgiveness of sins. And you will receive the gift of the Holy Spirit."_

4. The Word of God tells us to *forgive others* that have sinned against us.

In Matthew 18, Jesus told Peter about the parable of the unmerciful servant. A servant owed his master a million dollar debt. When asked about the debt, the servant said he was unable to repay him. That he needed more time to repay it. Instead of the master throwing him and this servant's family in debtor prison, he had mercy and forgave him of his debt.

This same servant then met up with someone who owed him a hundred dollar debt. When the other person told the servant that he could not pay the debt, the servant put him in jail instead of forgiving such a small debt like his master had forgiven him. This injustice was brought to the attention of the master, who called the servant and asked him why he could not forgive as he had forgiven him? This servant's selfishness and lack of mercy so angered the master that he threw him in jail until he paid back the entire million dollars that was owed.

Then Jesus said in *Matthew 18:.35, "This is how my heavenly Father will treat each of us unless you forgive your brother from your heart."*

In the Lord's Prayer, the Bible tells us in *Luke 11:4, "Forgive us our sins, for we also forgive everyone who sins against us."*

In *Ephesians 4:31-32*, the Bible tells us to, *"Get rid of all bitterness, rage and anger, brawling and slander, along with every form of malice. Be kind and compassionate to one another, forgiving each other, just as Christ God forgave you."*

Do you know your rights with God? In knowing where you stand with the Lord, no one can deceive you of your righteousness with God.

The Bible says in *Colossians 2:13-14*, *"When you were dead in your sins, and in the uncircumcision of your sinful nature, God made you alive with Christ. He forgave us all our sins, having canceled the written code, with its regulations, that was against us and that stood opposed to us; he took it away, nailing it on the cross."*

So my dear friend, do you now see how God forgives us of our sins? It is by us receiving His son Jesus Christ as our personal Savior, by confessing Him as Lord and repenting of our sins. *1 John 1:9 says that, "if we confess our sins, He is faithful to forgive us and cleanse us from all unrighteousness".* We also have to forgive those who have wronged us (forgive us our sins as we forgive those who sin against us). We also know that in accepting Jesus Christ, we have been made righteous with God through the blood of Jesus on the cross.

The Bible tells us that once our sins are forgiven, they are wiped out and canceled.

So once we have followed these steps in asking for forgiveness, why can't we forgive ourselves? By not forgiving ourselves, we are allowing the enemy to have dominion over our lives and our mind. He plays games on our minds to control us. Do not choose to allow the enemy this power. We have many blessings awaiting us. Therefore, by the grace of God and knowing our place with God, let us claim our minds and our lives back and allow God to do a good and new work

in us.

Chapter Two

HOW I OVER CAME MY PAST

"God is able to do exceedingly abundantly above all that we ask or think, according to the power that works in us."

(Ephesians 3:20)

At first, I did not want to share my own painful story. Even today it still stings a little bit. However, I know that God honors obedience. As a result, I am sure that someone special reading this book will arrive at the same liberating realization that they are not alone. Could that special someone be you?

I was born in Ghana, West Africa. At the age of three months old, (*according to my grandmothers account*), I was inflicted with a serious illness that almost killed me. They tried everything medical yet there was no hope. The doctors gave up on me and this discouraged my parents but not my grandmother. She turned to holistic medicine for a possible cure.

A relative brought a stranger over to meet my grandmother who had heard of my sickness. The stranger went with my grandmother to the woods of her backyard and showed her which trees to pick leaves off from. The stranger instructed my grandmother to blend the leaves into a cocktail. She was further instructed to use a dropper to drop some of the cocktail at various times into my nostrils. My grandmother did as such and followed the instructions exactly. A week later, I started to get better and within a month I was healed completely.

According to my grandmother, she had received a miracle. She went to church to testify and made sure everyone who would listen to her heard about it. My grandmother said she looked everywhere in the village to find the stranger to thank him and till today he was nowhere to be found. Little did we know then that God's healing power over my life was not just sheer luck! It was divinely orchestrated. Even then, God had his plans and had a call on my life to do his work, yet He was waiting for the appointed time.

My parents left me in the care of my grandmother when I was only one year old to venture outside of the country and seek a better lifestyle. So I grew up with very little memory of my mom and dad. They came to visit occasionally but not enough for me to establish a relationship with them. My early years were spent growing up longing every single day for my parent's love and affection. I could not wait until the day we became a unified family again. As a child, I did not understand the concept that my parents were away getting a better life for us. All I knew was that I felt lonely. My loneliness was worse when I saw other children with their parents.

Countless hours were spent dreaming of the day my parents would come for me.

Finally, the sweet day I had anticipated with every fiber of my being came when I was ten years old. My parents had found their better life and were living in the United States. An uncle and I journeyed over from Africa to live with them. Admittedly, this was a very difficult time for me. The arrangement was not quite how I had envisioned it during all those years. The reality was I did not know these complete strangers whom I called, "my parents". We had to learn to love each other. At first, I was very sad and longed for my family in Ghana because that was who I knew. That was my comfort zone. I tried very hard to be a good daughter but it was a challenge. I was sick at heart and consumed with feeling unloved and unwanted.

I found out I had two brothers that I did not know who were born in the United States of America while I lived in Ghana. The three of us needed to develop relationships with one another. I know my parents and family were trying but it was very difficult. It was worse when I got in trouble and was punished. I felt like these unfamiliar people hated me. In hindsight, that was not the case. But at the time, I continued to grow up with an unrequited longing for love and affection.

At sixteen years old, a young man whom I liked very much came into my life. I introduced him to my parents and my mom decreed that as long as we did not get sexually involved we could see each other with adult supervision.

I was very happy. I felt that what I was looking for was finally here. We dated for a while and did not get intimate until I was over eighteen years old. When I started college, the relationship fell apart. That devastated me because I believed he was the answer to my prayers for a life partner. I became withdrawn. It took a while for me to get over him, but I did and began dating again.

I still had that innate yearning for affection and love. The men that I met certainly sensed this about me. Although most felt that they could not fulfill this need, they nonetheless played on it to win my affection. As a result, I became pregnant several times and had abortions. No one was ever told of my pregnancies. My silence was rooted in the fear that if my parents found out then they would kill me. I also wanted to avoid disappointing them. Plus, I certainly did not want to bring a child into this world while I was not married. Once, I was so ashamed of my actions that I even contemplated taking my own life. Looking back, I recklessly took over the counter medications and engaged in excessive regimens that could have killed me. The thought that I was the most horrible and evil person alive was constantly in my mind.

I remember desperately crying out to God in prayer one day and asking to be forgiven of all my sins. I told God that if He did not allow me to have children anymore in my life then I would understand because of my sinful actions. In the middle of all of this upheaval I kept having a recurrent dream about seeing a beautiful baby boy. His tiny face was so vivid. Yet I did not understand the dream and it finally ceased after about six months. In my time of sorrow, matters were made worse when I also became aware of a repressed feeling of sexual abuse as a child. It was remote, and to this day I have not fully consciously evoked these feelings and cannot clearly understand them but I do know without a doubt that something did happen and I was inappropriately touched.

The weeks became months of these life trying ordeals. I decided it was better to stay by myself instead of taking someone else on this emotional roller coaster. Much of this time was spent reading a lot of spiritual books as well as some parts of the Bible. My parents used to take us to church but I did not have that personal relationship with God until the time I began reading and seriously studying about God, Jesus Christ and the Holy Spirit. I was like a dry sponge that had been given water. I wanted to soak everything in. I tried to seek God as much as I could. I went to church, gave my life to God and became a born again Christian by accepting the Lord Jesus Christ as my personal Savior.

Years later, after I met my husband and was married, my past sins continued to haunt me. I honestly thought that I would never have a baby. Imagine my amazement and unbridled joy when I conceived again. Despite complications, nine months later I gave birth to my first son. Out of a thankful heart, I rededicated him back to God. Several years later, the Lord blessed us again with another son. The Lord had showed me beyond any shadow of a doubt that He had forgiven me of my past sins but I was still not able to forgive myself. It was not until my second son was about six months old that the Lord reminded me of the recurrent dream that I had during the times of having the abortions. Then I looked intently at my second son's face. This was the same face of that little boy I had seen in my recurrent dream.

The fact is that I never could understand that dream back then. I did not "get" the connection to my second son. Then I prayed for the Lord to give me an interpretation of the dream. The Lord told me that He had forgiven me long ago and that He knew I had not forgiven myself so He had to give me something tangible. He knew when the time was right the recurrent dream would show me that He had forgiven me so I could now forgive myself. He said, "I showed you your son's face in the dream and now I am recalling the dream for you. So as you hold your son in your arms you can see that it is the same face that you saw many years ago. I have forgiven you so it is time to forgive yourself. Now you can better serve me without any hindrance." Upon hearing this I cried for days. Through my tears I finally prayed for God to specifically help me forgive myself.

Today, as I am writing this book I have forgiven myself. But that's not all there is. Through God's abundant mercies, I am also able to freely share my shameful past with you. Now, you can also be liberated by His mercy to be forgiven and receive all your blessings.

Remember those feelings of loneliness and void? God has clearly shown me that as I humbly submit to His will and allow Him to work His purpose in my life that I have overcome those feelings that caused me such strife. Since I let go and am not doing it by my own will and strength, those feelings of neediness and loneliness are gone.

I actually feel more satisfied, fulfilled, and happier. It was never about my parents, a life partner, or anyone else. This was about allowing God to do His work in me so I would find in Him that deep seated innate satisfaction, affection, and love I had been searching for so aimlessly. Only He can do that for us. To God be the Glory!

The Bible says: *"Be anxious for nothing, but in everything by prayer and supplication, with thanksgiving, let our requests be made known to God. And when we do the peace of God, which surpasses all understanding, will guard our hearts and minds through Christ Jesus." (Philippians 4:6-7).*

I now know that my parents loved me very much. They did not know how to be affectionate due to no fault of their own but rather as a result of their own upbringing and culture. They showed their love and support in other ways which became very apparent to me later on.

That elusive deep seated love and need I had longed for could only be fulfilled by the Lord Jesus Christ. Parents, there is a time for punishment and there is also a time for affection for your children. My prayer is that you show your children affection, love, and kindness so they do not seek it elsewhere. If you are struggling with this then ask God for a lenient heart.

Chapter Three

GOD'S FORGIVENESS IS MERCIFUL

In Acts 13:38, Peter said: "Therefore, my brothers, I want you to know that through Jesus the forgiveness of sins is proclaimed to you. Through him, everyone who believes is justified from everything you could not be justified from by the Law of Moses"

Ruth's Story

Ruth had always loved God and was considered a "good person" growing up. She grew to adulthood in a stable family. Both parents were hard working, educated and knew God. These same values were taught to their children.

When Ruth was in her early twenties, she met and fell deeply in love with a certain young man. They began to date then became engaged a few years later. Months before their wedding day Ruth took a fateful step to be closer to where he worked. She moved in with him and some of his family members. Soon thereafter, he broke the engagement and started mistreating her. Ruth returned to her family home hurt and disappointed. There she discovered she was pregnant and eventually gave birth to a beautiful baby boy.

With her parent's help, Ruth channeled her energy into continuing her education after her son was born. After completing her education a few years later she decided to start dating again. Those relationships were always unsuccessful for one reason or another. Then Ruth stopped dating again. A few years went by. Weary of loneliness and longing for companionship she launched out once more into the singles scene.

For the second time she met a young man and fell in love. Once again they moved in together intending to marry. As if predetermined to repeat past history, Ruth became pregnant again... this time giving birth to a daughter. The child's father wanted to get married. However, Ruth hesitated because she knew something was not quite right.

In reality, her lover was both a jealous and possessive man. His overly protective quality seemed cute at first because she desired attention and security. Ruth became more and more afraid as it spiraled downward into vicious emotional and verbal abuse. This pattern became so ominous that Ruth feared for her and her children's very lives.

Deep down she wanted the relationship to work out but couldn't ignore the warning signs. An innate feeling nudged her to let it go and move on. Ruth wisely left the relationship, albeit reluctantly. No mother deliberately chooses to feel the bite of disappointment and loneliness without a good reason like protecting her children. Not too long afterwards Ruth became withdrawn for a third time. Feeling like a complete failure, she struggled with issues of self-worth and depression like an inexperienced swimmer in deep water.

It took Ruth awhile to give love one last chance. Then she met Sam. He was completely different from any other man she had ever known. First of all, it did not matter to Sam that Ruth had children from previous relationships. How rare is that? To Ruth's credit, she was careful not to repeat the same mistakes that she had made in her previous relationships. That was wisdom because Sam genuinely loved her and her children very much. Before meeting Sam, she decided that she was not going to have any more children. After they were married, Ruth reversed her decision because Sam had no children of his own. Soon she was pregnant. Nine months later Ruth and Sam were blessed with a beautiful baby girl.

Shortly after the birth of his daughter, Sam became distant and withdrawn. He wasn't as attentive as he had been previously. Ruth felt that something was not right with her marriage. Eventually, it was found out that Sam was cheating on her. Ruth was understandably upset and overcome with emotion. Her first inclination was to run away and leave the marriage because this was the coping pattern of her life.

Ruth finally confided in me and we prayed together. I gently advised Ruth to personally let go of the fight and trust the Lord completely for justice. I shared my belief that this fight was not her fight but God's fight. We asked God to bring sense to all the insanity that was going on and mend her breaking heart. After that prayer of agreement, Ruth calmly confronted Sam and he openly confessed everything to her. He was remorseful and expressed sincere regret. By taking full accountability for what he had done, Sam took the first steps to repair the broken marriage in order for it to succeed.

But Ruth also put blame on herself because she could not grant grace and forgive the fact that she had two children from two different failed relationships. So sad but true. This unforgiveness from her past mistakes was hindering her from receiving many blessings in both her present and future.

Is there something that you need to forgive within yourself?

Now Sam and Ruth and their children have begun attending church together and are pursuing a closer relationship with God. Their marriage is going to take a lot of work, effort, trust and forgiveness in order to become stronger but with God impossible things are made possible. If you put God first in every aspect of life then God will deal with you accordingly.

God sent this young man with no children of his own to come and help Ruth. God gave her to Sam so that he could have children of his own. That was His good plan for both of their lives. Because Sam did not have a personal relationship with God, he lacked the moral strength to overcome sexual temptation so he fell prey to it. Ruth, through prayer gave it all to God, and through God's mercy turned a negative situation into something positive. God's love and grace eventually drew them to church. Now they will forever be guided by Him. The fact is our Holy and Omnipotent God intimately knows your heart. He has good plans for your life, too.

Ruth and Sam are human beings just like you and I. The Bible clearly states that "all have sinned and fallen short of the glory of God". However, if we depend on God then He will always direct us back to the right path.

My prayer is that Ruth's story will help both men and women confronted by similar life circumstances to turn to God and allow Him to work graciously in them.

"For Christ died for sins once for all, the righteous for the unrighteous, to bring you to God." (1 Peter 3:18).

Chapter Four

BREAKING GENERATIONAL CURSE
THROUGH GOD'S GRACE

"In Him we have redemption through His blood, the forgiveness of sins, in accordance with the riches of God's grace."

(Ephesians 1:7).

Sarah's Story

Sarah was born into a loving family but for years she has kept a terrible secret from her parents. Beginning at a very tender age and lasting through eighth grade, Sarah was molested by a very close family member. No one was ever told of her horrific ordeal. The abuse with that family member has stopped but Sarah was left emotionally scarred. Tragically, she allowed abuse in various forms to continue throughout high school by different individuals. As a result, Sarah almost committed suicide then but was saved by a loyal friend.

After high school, Sarah moved to a bigger city thinking life would be better. Life actually worsened for Sarah... she had not dealt with her pain and the injustice done to her so she had a very low self esteem. This low self esteem attracted the wrong type of men towards Sarah and landed her into many negative situations. During one of these unhealthy relationships she was introduced to drugs and alcohol. Her life spiraled downward with drugs as she turned to lying, stealing, and other criminal activities.

Sarah was painfully aware of how low her life had become but didn't know how to turn it around. She experienced major depression and feelings of worthlessness. She believed she was an utter failure. Sarah even developed a multiple personality disorder so she would not have to deal with the reality of her life. Thoughts of ending her life came easily and often. The abusive relationship (both verbally and physically) that she was in offered no way out. Sarah felt that returning to her parents wasn't an option because they would be disappointed with her. She treaded along life on thin ice and then moved back to her abusive partner until he was sent to jail.

In a moment of clarity despite an ongoing drug habit, Sarah finally moved back home with her parents. Then she found out she was pregnant.

One day as she was sitting down, Sarah pulled something long out of her nostrils, looked at it and said, "I have got to stop." Right then she fell to her knees, praying and crying out to God. The very next Sunday she went to church and gave her life to Christ. Although, her problems did not disappear right away, she felt an overwhelming sense of peace in her life. The irony of Sarah's story is that she was going to church during the ordeals throughout her life. Yet she didn't have a personal relationship with God. What is even more interesting was that she always felt a presence of divine protection in her life.

There are many people who attend church and sit in the sanctuary every service feeling all alone. They feel like they have nowhere to turn. They are lost and hurting. *Can you identify them where you fellowship?*

Or are you one of them?

Could it be that there is more than just merely sitting in church? What about your relationship with God? Are you seeking a closer relationship with Him? You can begin by accepting the Lord Jesus Christ as your personal Savior. The Bible states that no man comes to the Father (in relationship) except through the Son. In doing so, you will find fulfillment and purpose for your life.

Today, Sarah has such a strong relationship with the Lord because she has been forgiven of her sins. He guides her in every decision she makes because she prays first and acts after hearing His answer. Then she is obedient and does exactly what she was told to do. With God's help Sarah has forgiven her abusers and herself. She is always being thankful for God's mercy and receives continual blessings in her life. Now she expresses that grateful heart as a praise and worship team leader, singing in the choir.

Sarah introduced her children to church and the victorious Christian life so they will not fall into the same life patterns as she did. By God's grace, her children have developed their own personal relationships with Jesus Christ and He is now guiding them along the path of righteousness.

Do you see God's mercy and glory in all of this? The people that abused Sarah were probably also abused themselves. There was a generational curse of abuse and dysfunction that had been passed down her bloodline. God's almighty power breaks the curse of all sin forever. By showing favor to Sarah and saving her and her children from sin, He has ended the impact of the generational curse in this family forever and ever.

My friend, what the Lord has done for Sarah can also be done for you. The Lord is abundant in all things. All you have to do is ask and He will answer. Knock and the door will be opened to you. Seek and you will find Him. He knows how you have been afflicted and what you are going through. He can turn it all around for you. He promises to turn your mourning into dancing. Trade Him your pain and sorrow for joy and gladness. He is the only one that can make everything right. You can trust Him.

Let us pray:

Dear God,

I am hurting so much. I am lost in my life. I have no idea where to turn or what to do. The only thing I know to do is to pray to you. Please forgive me of all of the things I have done wrong and continue to do wrong. Please help me forgive those who have caused me pain. Allow those whom I have caused pain to also forgive me. I am in a dark place right now in my life and I need your light to shine on me to see me through it all. See me through this and I will commit my life to serving you and doing the things that will bring you glory. Please save me and have mercy on me for I am lost. I am so wounded that I cannot even pray effectively so please be with me and work on me so that I can give you all the glory. I thank you God for hearing me!

Amen!

Chapter Five

THE EFFECT OUR PARENTS' CHOICES HAVE ON US

"Train up a child in the way he should go; even when he is old he will not depart from it."

Proverbs 22:6

Hope in God

If you have been hurt by your parents or caretakers then please pray and allow God to heal your heart. You have the power of choice to change what will happen from now on. Your earthly parents may have disappointed you but your Heavenly Father will not. God is always good and has good plans for your life. He can turn <u>all</u> your heartaches and pains into victories.

Do not allow that pain or hurt to fester and infect you. You will avoid things like depression, feeling worthless, alcoholism, drug abuse, overeating, abuse or criminal activity. Otherwise, these negative consequences could control your future and be passed along to your children and their children. Your prayers and forgiveness of those who offended you release God's healing virtue into your heart and memory. He will transform that hurting experience into a better way to live. You will make better life choices. Those choices will ultimately positively affect your children and their children. God's blessings will overflow from you into your children and grandchildren.

Consider this. It is a well known fact that children of alcoholic parents grow up in dysfunctional family household. They are more likely to become alcoholics like their parents and continue the pattern of dysfunction in their families. Accepting Jesus Christ as your personal Savior and submitting to Him is the first step to overcoming any addiction and accompanying dysfunctional behavior. The Holy Spirit will intervene and change you from the inside out. Alcohol will taste awful. His Word (the Bible) will teach you a better way to live. The end result is you become a better person than your parents or caretakers were to you.

God knew you before you were even conceived by your parents. He knew when you were going to be born. He knows exactly when you are appointed to die. He knows in advance of all the trials, tribulations and happiness that you are going to encounter in life. He allows (not causes) events to happen so that you will have Godly character and He can be glorified. A Biblical example of this is in the Book of Job. God allowed Satan to bring terrible pain and suffering upon Job and his family to prove that Job was a faithful man. Despite the intense trials and tribulations that he endured in that hard season of life, Job's faith was not shaken nor did he abandon God.

God's Word promises that you are not here by chance or coincidence. Your life has purpose and meaning. You have real significance. Because God is truth and cannot lie then you can completely trust and have faith in Him for every circumstance of life. Don't we most often go to God when we are facing some adversity in our life? Doesn't He graciously help to resolve this adversity in our life or shows us the way to overcome it? Afterwards, if we are faithful then we give Him the glory. Victorious living is always for His glory. The testimony we share brings advancement of His kingdom as it ministers to others.

Here's a scenario of parents who have made a positive impact on their children's lives. They attend church with their children, pray with them on a daily basis and introduce them to God at an early age. Proverbs says "Train up a child in the ways of the Lord and they shall not depart from them." Children from homes like these will always be directed back to the path of righteousness even if they take a detour to create their own testimony. This establishment of faith in their children will also carry on to their future generations. These are the kind of Godly parents we should aspire to become.

This truth is worth repeating. Our parent's choices can either have a negative or positive effect on us. Their choices can dictate the path that we take if we allow them to. However, we don't have to allow their poor choices to affect us negatively because as Christians, we are children of a loving Heavenly Father. We are joint heirs with Jesus in His Father's Kingdom. Therefore, God is for you no matter what shame or affliction has been thrust upon you. It was not and is not your fault. Receive salvation, by believing and accepting His son Jesus Christ, pour out your heart to Him and allow Him to do a new work in you so you can write a new history for His glory.

Unfortunately, there are children who are being abused – mentally, verbally, physically, and sexually. Many times this comes by the hand of a family member or loved one. Often these children suffer in silence because they are afraid no one will believe them. Some fear for their very lives or the lives of their loved ones. My heart breaks and I am sure it breaks yours to think that such cruel torture happens but it does. I pray to our God who is omniscient, omnipotent, and omnipresent to expose such evil deeds. That He delivers these perpetrators to justice and by His grace forces them to face their sins. Then in His mercy cause them to repent so they will not hurt another child.

Lisa's Story

Lisa was born to an alcoholic mother. When Lisa's mother married Lisa's father, she already had four children from a previous relationship. Her new marriage produced three more children. Lisa's biological father tried hard to tolerate his wife's drinking habit but at some point he just couldn't take it anymore and left the marriage. Lisa's mother eventually married again. She had one more child for a total of eight children. Lisa soon found herself living with her mother and stepfather plus the four youngest siblings after the oldest three left home. Her stepfather started abusing Lisa and her other siblings when she was about five years old. Lisa and her sister Dora were not only sexually molested but verbally and physical abused. Her brother was mentally, verbally, and physically abused. Her oldest sister was sexually, verbally, and physically abused. The stepfather was able to attack them after getting their alcoholic mother so drunk she was unaware of what was going on. This pattern of abuse continued in the family until Lisa was just about age nine.

The abuse ceased because her brother was old enough to threaten to beat and kill the step father if he ever touched him or his siblings again. Throughout their ordeal, the siblings bonded and depended on each other. The children eventually told their aunt but were told not to tell anyone. Her contention was, "Whatever happens in a family stays in a family. She would deal with it later." Lisa believes this aunt did inform her mother about the abuse but nothing was ever done about it.

When Lisa was twelve, she dearly missed her biological father but he was remarried. His new wife (who was also an alcoholic) did not want Lisa or her brothers and sisters around their Dad. As a result of her influence, he neglected his children. Lisa's sister was so wounded by their abuse and the paternal neglect that she channeled her lack of love and parental guidance into seeking love from different men. She first became pregnant at fifteen then again at sixteen. She was lost and constantly lived on the street.

While the abuse was going on, Lisa would protect Dora as best as she could. After seeing what was happening to her now and not wanting for history to repeat itself, Lisa began to care for those children. She recalls going to school and work then coming back home to care for them. During her absence she would pay a neighbor to take care of Dora's little ones until she returned. Lisa gave her heart to the Lord during this very active time at the tender age of fifteen. Lisa feels that God's protection was on her because there was one thing her alcoholic mother did right. She had each of her children dedicated to the Lord in Baptism and sent to Catholic school where they received a solid education based on Christian teaching.

When Lisa reached adulthood at twenty one, all her siblings and Dora's children left the house with her to seek a better life. By then they all had accepted Jesus Christ as their personal Savior. They prayed for the Lord to help them forgive their parents and their abuser. Today they are totally free from their bondage.

The abusive stepfather is now deceased. Because of God's abundant healing in forgiveness, Lisa and Dora lovingly took care of him as he was dying of cancer. This man who had abused them in the past was compassionately attended to by his victims until the day he died. What a transformation! In mercy he was told by his victims that they had forgiven him. Lisa and Dora helped him pray to accept Jesus Christ as his personal Savior and ask for God's forgiveness before he died. He then confessed his own unspeakable past as a victim of sexual, mental, verbal and physical abuse after being adopted. This is a prime example of how _good_ triumphs over evil in God's Kingdom.

So you see my dear friend, their stepfather never dealt with his pain and the past offenses committed against him. He didn't know any better. So this abomination carried forward into his adult life and negatively affected the next generation. But God in His mercy helped Lisa and Dora break this "generational curse" because of their willingness to forgive. Glory to the God who saves us and make us brand new by being born again. By graciously mending our broken hearts from the pains and hurts in our lives, He enables us to forgive in order to move on from glory to glory.

_Let's share the words in "Footprints"_by Mary Stevenson which is one of Lisa's favorite writings:_

One night I had a dream.

I dreamt I was walking along the beach with the Lord and across the sky flashed scenes from my life. For each scene I noticed two sets of footprints, one belonged to me and the other to the Lord. When the last scene of my life flashed before me, I looked back at the footprints in the sand.

I noticed that many times along the path of my life, there was only one set of footprints. I also noticed that it happened at the very lowest and saddest times in my life. This really bothered me and I questioned the Lord about it. "Lord, you said that once I decided to follow you, you would walk with me all the way, but I have noticed that during the most troublesome times in my life there is only one set of footprints." "I don't understand why in times when I needed you most, you should leave me." The Lord replied, "My precious, precious child, I love you and would never leave you during your times of trial and suffering."

"When you saw only one set of footprints, it was then that I carried you."

Let us pray:

Dear Father,

I am praying this prayer because I have been afflicted in a negative way by my parents or a guardian that has left an intangible hole in my heart. I know that it is only in believing in you and your ways that I will find the answers and direction to what I am searching for. In changing my path from the negative downward spiral to a more positive future, I know this is what I need. Please heal my heart, help me to forgive and help me not to transfer this negative energy and flow to my children and grandchildren. Without you, I know I cannot do this. With you, I know the impossible can become possible. Thank you for healing me. May you receive the glory! Amen!

The Bible says in *Colossians 1:13-14, "For He has rescued us from the dominion of darkness and brought us into the kingdom of the Son He loves, in whom we have redemption, the forgiveness of sins."*

Chapter Six

UNFORGIVENESS CAN KEEP US IN BONDAGE

"Be anxious for nothing, but in everything by prayer and supplication, with thanksgiving let our requests be made known to God. And when we do the peace of God, which surpasses all understanding will guard our hearts and minds through Christ Jesus."

(Philippians 4:6-7).

Mary's Story

Mary is a lovely woman who stayed in a state of unforgiveness for a very long time. She married her first husband when she was just a young woman. They had two beautiful daughters. The rocky relationship between Mary and her husband caused her to be very unhappy. At first she felt underappreciated then later unloved by this man. She eventually decided that he had to leave the marriage and move on to start a fulfilling new life with her daughters.

When Mary was dealing with serious issues in her marriage, there was another couple (Adam and Jane) who were friends with her and her husband. This couple was also having marital problems. Adam and Mary had already been friends, and in time their respective spouses became friends as well. Adam opened up about his unhappy marriage to Mary. As she listened with understanding, Mary encouraged Adam to do everything he could to make his marriage work.

Eventually, Mary also started confiding in Adam about her marital woes. Both Adam and Mary grew closer together from consoling each other as each of their marriages fell apart. Then one day, Adam told Mary that he had fallen in love with her. Adam also told his wife (Jane) that he was in love with Mary. Adam made it clear that he wanted out of his marriage since it was already falling apart.

To her credit, Mary did everything in her power to fight off the feelings and desires. She prayed for strength as well as kept her distance from Adam. But it was way too late because she was also in love with Adam. Both marriages ultimately ended in failure. Mary and Adam were married sometime later. Needless to say, there was a lot of blame assigned to Mary and Adam for the divorces. The fact was, their marriages were in their final stages of demise and were not going to survive anyway. Everyone needs a scapegoat.

As I am writing this book, Adam and Mary have been happily married for over ten years and still going strong. Mary's first husband is also happily married. Jane is still stuck in the past with blame and anger and refuses to get married because she is still waiting for her husband to come back. Mary had been living with guilt for the longest time because she felt terrible for falling in love with a man who was married at the time. She blames herself for the couple losing all their friends and even some close family members.

When I met Mary, she had this heavy burden on her heart. I prayed with her and asked her to pray for forgiveness. She did, and I know God has forgiven her, but Mary could not forgive herself. Then we prayed another prayer for God and the Holy Spirit to allow Mary to forgive herself and let go of the past. It took some time, but Mary has finally stopped blaming and has forgiven herself. She has a brighter outlook on life now. She can now see her many blessings and thanks God everyday for them.

Now that she knows God, she is praying for God to heal and soften the hearts of the close family members that they lost. She is optimistic that they all will be a family again. With God all things are possible. Mary will have her testimony someday after all she has endured.

What is most important is Adam, Mary, and the kids now have a stronger relationship with God. One day soon Mary's story will also inspire someone else who is in a similar situation to heal and forgive themselves. Forgiving yourself reaps many benefits. First, it allows you to develop a deeper relationship with God. Second, it frees you to seek and to live in His perfect will. Third, you can't help but become a blessing to others.

I also pray that Jane will finally let go of the past hurt and allow God to heal her so that she does not block herself from the many blessings and opportunities that God has for her life.

I keep emphasizing that you should give it all to God because if you do not then the end result can be devastating.

The Bible says: *"if we confess our sins, He is faithful and just to forgive us our sins and to cleanse us from all unrighteousness."* *(1 John 1:9).*

A Story With An Unfortunate Ending

I know a couple who to the outside world had it all. From all outside appearances they had a good marriage, children, good jobs and a beautiful home. Then one day the husband suddenly committed suicide. What a tragedy! The husband had an affair and felt so guilty that he could not forgive himself.

His suicide not only took away his life but his pain. That same act created much pain for those he left behind. If he had known God personally then he could have prayed for forgiveness for his adultery. He could've also asked for his wife's forgiveness. He would have experienced God's forgiveness and in time been able to forgive himself. Instead, the devil was able to trick him into believing that he was the most evil and volatile person alive.

Can you imagine the pain and loneliness he must have experienced before deciding to take his life? He had family and friends who adored him. The enemy made him believe in lies at his most vulnerable moment. It was a lie that he had no one to go to because God is always there. It was a lie that if he shared his story then he would be judged too negatively.

He left behind a hurt and broken wife. His children are doomed to grow up without their father. Certain family members and friends have lost a great person. Look at how many lives have been affected. From this one terrible mistake the enemy was able to control the mind of one person then encourage him to kill himself, yet all he had to do was give it all to God and let him do a new work in him for His glory.

"Therefore this is what the Lord says, 'If you repent, I will restore you that you may serve me." (Jeremiah 15:19).

Chapter Seven

OBEDIENCE TO YOUR CALLING

"I can do everything through Christ who strengthens me"

(Philippians 4:13)

How did I get here?

I am a practicing physician who is grateful to God for allowing me to serve in this capacity. As unbelievable as it may seem, I felt a sense of something missing in my life. I was not content. There had to be more. So I started searching for what the more could be. During this time, my family relocated from New York City to Dublin, a very small rural town in Georgia. Why move to Dublin from New York City? Now I understand that this was part of Gods' plan.

My husband Osei and our son moved to Dublin right after I finished my residency medical training. My training program was in Internal Medicine and I did it in New York City. In my heart I knew that I wanted to move to Atlanta, GA because I had fallen in love with the area after several visits to a friend who lived there. My husband and I began prayerfully considering a position in Dublin, GA. We felt that since Dublin was only two hours south of Atlanta, it would not be a bad commute if we wanted to visit. I can vividly remember praying about it by myself. God laid it on my heart to go for He had some souls for us to touch. I was obedient and moved forward in the application process. After an interview, I was offered and accepted the job. Then with some anxiety as well as excitement left our family in NYC and moved to Dublin, GA where we knew no one.

Within three months my husband and I both regretted our decision. We wished we had not moved. I prayed that God would allow us to go to a different place. The answer every time was, "It was not time yet and when the time came that He would let us know." We waited as we continued with our daily lives. Sometimes the waiting period is the hardest. Our family was blessed with another son while we were in waiting mode. God was right! We touched many lives in Dublin and many lives touched us. We kept on praying. Five years passed before He gave us the okay to move on. One year later we finally made the move to Atlanta, GA.

My undergraduate degree was in Biochemistry. While still practicing medicine full time, I used those skills as a Biochemist to formulate my own line of skincare products. A lot of time and money was invested producing and marketing this skincare line but with very little results. I was making a lot of money with my job as a physician and several other businesses but very little money was staying in my hands at the end of the day. I knew something was not right and felt a nudging "to let go and let God."

Then one day in desperation, I broke down and actually cried out to God. I told Him that I wanted His perfect will and purpose to be done in my life. Miraculously, God answered by my finding a book called *"Praying God's Will for Your Life"* by Stormie Omartian. Each sentence was read as attentively and diligently as if I were studying for my medical school board exams. There was much practical insight that I gained from its pages. It confirmed that I had been trying to do all the good works by my own effort and strength without allowing God His proper place. I had known for a very long time that there was the call of ministry on my life. The fact was I had been running away from it. You know what I have learned? You can run only from God for just so long. Then at His appointed time and place, you can run no more. This revelation came to me as my husband and children had relocated from Dublin to Atlanta, GA. Our family was in the midst of getting adjusted to our new environment and God was dealing seriously with me.

We were living together in Atlanta but my job as a physician was two hours and forty-five minutes away in Eastman, GA. I would go down for a few days at a time to work then come back home with my ever so supportive husband caring for our two boys and our home. It was on one of my first few trips to Eastman, GA that I began to read *"Praying God's Will For Your Life"*. I knew without a doubt that the ministry I had been running away from was about to burst forth like a flower in bloom. I simply did not know what the ministry was... yet.

I remember praying and asking God, "How can I minister to others and teach them when I personally do not know the Bible that well?" The Lord told me, "Not to doubt no matter what I would be told." He also said, "I am to write a book." This book specifically, then He gave me the exact wording for the title.

I argued with the Lord, "But I am not a writer. If I don't know the Bible that well then how can I write a book?" The Lord assured me that He would give me all the help I needed. Plus the resources as well as the skilled people necessary along the way to make this book happen.

In obedience I slowly began writing down whatever came into my mind regarding forgiveness. Then I asked God to give me a sure sign that it really was Him who wanted me to make this a book about forgiving ourselves. He instantly answered. I am not kidding you. The following really happened to me. Another book was on my lap as I had interrupted my reading and prayed that prayer. When I resumed reading, the very next three chapters were about forgiveness. I said, "Thank you Lord but I am still not sure".

The next day a fellow physician friend came to visit me while I worked. She is also a minister of the Gospel. I confided in her that God was leading me to write a book on forgiveness even though I didn't understand the reason why. When I revealed the title that God had given for this book she said, "Jacqueline, maybe there is something hidden in you that God wants you to share with the world so that it can be a help to many other persons." "But what could it be?" I responded sharply but stopped speaking because suddenly I knew what God wanted me to share.

As I proceeded to relate my hard experiences, my friend didn't judge or chastise me. She just simply said, "God wants you to share your story." "But I can't share this story with the world. It is too shameful." I tried to defend myself. Then I was informed that she was going to bring me a book that would help shed light on God's plans for me. When we met a short time later, I was given *"Your Scars are Beautiful to God"* by Sharon Jaynes.

Sharon Jaynes' book transformed my life and made everything crystal clear to me. That is when I got on my knees and said, "God, I am ready. Use me as you wish." After reading her book I was able to sincerely request God's Healing for the very first time. Healing from those hurts allowed me to forgive others who have caused me pain. Being healed also allows me to ask others that I have hurt to forgive me.

Only by *God's* grace was I willing to tell you my story. Really, I'm just a vessel that God is using so that He can help others and demonstrate His glory and mercy. This is why I am sharing my story with you.

What is your story? God will use it to heal others if you will let Him. I pray that He gives you the wisdom to ask for forgiveness when you sin and fall short of His glory. That He grants the peace you need to forgive yourself and others who may have hurt you. That your story will heal and restore others, just like *"Your Scars are Beautiful to God"*, did for me.

1 Corinthians 13:5 says that *"real love keeps no record of wrongs."*

Caution. Watch out when you do it on your own.

Success! We all know people who have "made it" in worldly terms. How often is it that people who have achieved this level of success have tragically fallen and lost everything? Some of these people did not know God. Others may have known God but did not allow God to do it for them. Perhaps some allowed God but did not give the credit and glory to God.

Just because you are successful in attaining your career goal or even your lifetime goal does not mean that you are fulfilling what your true calling or destiny is. You can't really know that without inquiring of God to define your true calling, purpose, and perfect will in your life. Devoid of God, it does not matter what your level of achievement or accomplishment is. Without Him there will always be an emptiness and a yearning for more. If you do not believe me, then consider this.

You've heard of successful people with a lot of money, fame, and power who either take their own lives or fell prey to some kind of temptation. The end result is disgrace. This is a life void of the constant indwelling of God and His Holy Living. Our present day society shamelessly exalts celebrities or people with status and power to the point of making the "have nots" crazy with envy. Some of these same people are constantly battling depression, promiscuity, sadness, hopelessness, substance abuse, criminal activities and much more. This confirms the fact that money and power will never buy true happiness. That only comes by living a life that is aligned with God's perfect will.

On the flip side, we all know people who do not have much in the way of riches and power. Some are men and women of God who start churches from scratch. They invest their time, money and energy to win souls for God. Sometimes they struggle to pay their monthly bills. By faith they depend upon the God that has called them and allow Him to do His work through them for His own glory. I have had the privilege of meeting some of these great men and women of God. Seeing their level of happiness and contentment in the Lord despite adversities is priceless.

As I have mentioned before, I am a medical doctor. I am blessed by God to have had the privilege to accomplish this goal in my life. However, as my life progressed there came a time in my life where I was making a lot of money as a physician but I felt a void. There was an emptiness that I could not explain. I needed more. I felt in my spirit that the calling on my life was more than being a medical doctor.

So I started to pray for God to reveal His perfect will and purpose in my life and the lives of my immediate family. Throughout all this, I loved God dearly with all my heart but I was doing it with my own will. God granted me His permissive will to continue but what I was missing in my spirit was the fulfillment that only comes from being in His *perfect* will.

The end result was not pretty... too much debt. God finally captured my attention when my husband and I lost over fifty thousand dollars on a business venture in a single day. I couldn't eat, sleep or pray. We were devastated. I shared my situation with my best friend who is also a woman of God. She said, "Even if you cannot pray then just *talk* to God. He will hear you. He created you and knows your heart. He will provide for your every need." That is exactly what I did. I just had a conversation with God.

The issue before me was now that He had my attention, would I do what he has called me to do? I replied, "Lord, did it have to take this amount of loss to capture my attention?" With love He said, "You were so deep into making money and thinking you were in control of your destiny that you did not need Me. So I had to find a way to say slow down and hear Me out." Well, it worked because I was ready to hear Him, listen, and obey.

What came out of my willingness to listen and pay attention to God's calling was this book. You see, God will do things and capture your attention in obscure ways sometimes. It's not just for you but to fulfill His perfect will and purpose in you. This He does for His glory and the expansion of His kingdom. My friend, pursue God in revealing His perfect will and purpose in your life with the same zeal that you have when you are pursuing a business venture that will profit you.

I promise that discovering your destiny from God far outweighs any monetary gain you may acquire.

If you still doubt me, test God and see if He will not use you as a vessel to manifest the purpose of your life for His glory. Pray and ask Him to reveal to you what His perfect will and purpose is for your life. Wait and you will see miracles flow in your life. Make sure to give *Him* the glory for all your blessings.

Chapter eight

THE POWER OF WORDS

"God is able to do exceedingly abundantly above all that we ask or think, according to the power that works in us."

(Ephesians 3:20).

The Power of Words

Words are powerful. Negative words can leave a long damaging impression on a young person's life. Positive words can uplift a young life and pull him or her through some of life's most difficult and challenging situations.

Example #1

I was a very good student in college and excelled in the sciences. However, I was not as confident when it came to grammar and writing. Perhaps, it was because English was not my first language. I took a course in English Comprehension and on one assignment we had to write a story. I wrote the story and turned it in. I thought it was well written and was very happy with the finished work.

My professor had an entirely different assessment. He severely criticized my work. I was coldly informed that I was not a "writer." His harsh and negative review of my writing left such a lasting impression on me that I refused to ever take another writing class or write for anyone ever again. To this day, I cannot recall his name. His utter contempt left such a negative perception of myself in regard to writing that when God spoke to my heart I said, "But why me? I cannot write." If I did not have the faith that I have now by God's grace then I would have missed out on my calling and blessing. Such is the power that negative words can have on a person's life when not tactfully delivered.

Example #2

There was a meeting I had with an academic counselor when I was doing my Master's program where I expressed my strong desire to attend medical school. He advised me not to enroll because admission to medical school was very difficult. That pessimistic attitude caused me to be discouraged for a little while. I thought seriously about giving up until an old college friend called and suggested a medical school that she felt strongly I should apply to. I promptly mailed the application and was asked to interview. In the end, I was admitted without any difficulty to that particular medical school. That is another example of how I could have missed out on a blessing from God. Can you see how easily discouragement could've deterred me from my destiny?

Example #3

My mom has always been my rock. My backbone, too. She is not really a very affectionate person yet she is always encouraging to me. My mother has been my most priceless cheerleader. She encourages me again and again that I can become anything my heart desires as long as I am determined and persistent. My father used to always remind me that, "with God all things are possible." I remember these words of encouragement and keep pushing ahead to make progress towards my goal whenever I get into a situation that is difficult. If I hit a road block then I search until I find a way around it that keeps me moving closer to my goal.

Recently my youngest son Michael had just started kindergarten and was learning how to write. He adores his oldest brother Matthew and thinks he is the smartest child out there. He came crying to me hysterically one day and I asked, "Baby, what is wrong?" He replied, "Mama, I cannot do it." Instantly I recalled those words of encouragement my parents always had for me. So I said, "Michael, you can do all things as long as you believe you can. Mama knows you can do it. So you go on and prove Mama right." I saw his beautiful eyes light up as I wiped the tears from his face. He kept on going and continued his writing with a new found energy.

Michael looks up to his brother Matthew. He sees Matthew doing all this cool stuff so he feels that he needs to be just like his big brother. Michael is three years younger than Matthew and not at his brother's intellectual level yet. But Michael doesn't see it that way. That is what caused the discouragement when he felt that he could not write as well as Matthew. Those encouraging words spoken into Michael's spirit transformed him. He instantly began believing in his ability to write at his own his level.

Can you see how the power of encouraging words is working in your life or that of your loved ones? Do you understand how a positive mental attitude and self-image can carry them through their life's journey? Or your own?

Chapter Nine

COMMUNICATION IN MARRIAGE

"Whatever things you ask for in prayer, believing, you will receive."

(Matthew 21:22),

"if two of you agree on earth concerning anything that they ask, it will be done for them by my Father in heaven. For where two or three are gathered in My name, I am there in the midst of them."

(Matthew 18:19-20).

Don't we all get angry and hurt at one time or another? Shouldn't we be aware of the words we use when we are angry? We can easily say things we will regret later like hurtful words that cut deeply into someone's soul. This has happened to me. Words spoken in anger almost destroyed my marriage.

There was a time in my life where the enemy was attacking my marriage. My husband and I were constantly bickering over one issue or the other. He said words to me and I was hurt by them because I felt that he did not understand me. I did not respond right away with forgiveness but kept that hurt prisoner in my heart. The enemy saw this and he had his doorway into me.

Once we resumed the argument, I remembered the very words he had said. The pain and hurtful feelings flooded back into my being. I became even more angry and emotional. Then I hurled some of the most vicious and venomous verbiage imaginable at my husband. I no longer saw the man that I loved with all my heart. He was now the despicable enemy and not fit to remain in my presence. It was time to counterattack. But I was only aware of my pain so I lashed out like a cornered animal.

He was so hurt and wounded by my words that it almost cost me my marriage. Even after I apologized, he could not forgive me because the devil had him believing in a lie. I cried a lot and prayed to God. I confessed my sins and asked for forgiveness. God forgave me and I felt a peace within me, but my husband still would not forgive me. Then he stopped listening to me. My only course was to beg God to mend my husband's broken heart and remove his hurt. Only after a touch from God could he then find the willingness in his heart to forgive me.

It took some time but he eventually forgave me and we worked together to mend our marriage. The Holy Spirit had done His work in him to bring healing and forgiveness. The Holy Spirit also did a number on me. I was convicted of speaking the negative and destructive words that proceeded out of _my_ mouth. I learned that although the tongue is a small organ, it can be one of the most damaging weapons that a human can use. Read in the Bible, James Chapter 3 then consider the following verse:

"Be kind and compassionate to one another, forgiving each other, just as in Christ, God forgave you." (Ephesians 4:32)

Do you see how the enemy was able to simultaneously feed on both my husband's and my hurts? Didn't he invade us to the point that the very words coming out of our mouths were like a wildfire destroying everything in its path? The enemy also had dominion over our minds and hearts via our hurts. Without prayer and God's mercy, we almost did not forgive each other (a big sin). But to the Glory of God our beautiful marriage didn't end in divorce.

Marriage is an institution that is precious and beautiful to God. It is one of the most commonly attacked targets by the enemy. Two individuals from different backgrounds and upbringings become one. That unity creates a brand new and unique family background for the next generation. Each person has been independent in their own life prior to being married and is set in their own comfort zones. Getting married does not mean you become a different person. You decide to make adjustments in order to better accommodate your mate. It takes commitment and determination by both mates to forge a brand new life together that makes a marriage work.

First and foremost, put God first in order to overcome the many hurricanes that occur in marriage. Constant prayer, love and forgiveness are necessary. God always brings hope when we encounter difficult times. Reading other

Christian books and resources teaching on marriage, in addition to reading the Word of God together will guide you into a deeper understanding of what God recognizes as a successful marriage.

For those of us who are married, we have to make a conscious effort to place our marriages into God's hands. We should pray for our marriages and mates on a daily basis. We should pray for God to strengthen our love for each other, protect us from temptation, anger, afflictions, our finances, and conflict resolution. We should ask daily for wisdom in our dealings with our husbands and wives. Both in times of conflict, as well as happy times. (Do you remember, "for better or for worse?") Many issues are bound to come up in marriage that could have negative outcomes if we allow it. By faith, we have the power to prophesy good outcomes by speaking good words into those issues.

By giving it all to God, we allow Him to do a new work in us. He will mend our broken hearts, calm us when we are angry, comfort us in time of sorrow and give us wisdom when we are at our wits end concerning our marriage. If your mate has not received salvation then lead him or her by demonstrating Christ's love. Pray and allow God to do the rest. You cannot change your spouse's mind or attitudes. But God can and does in response to your fervent prayer.

Communication is very important in a marriage. There is much to be said about spouses who communicate without attacking one another. The Bible tells us not to go to bed angry. If you are angry with your spouse then ask God to remove that anger from you. I have done this very thing many times. I will go into my little closet to pray and ask God for peace. It is quite amazing! After I pray my anger usually disappears.

Sometimes I get "reminded" afterwards by a nudge in my spirit that my anger has gone. It took me awhile to get into the habit of using this strategy. I used to communicate by yelling when I was hurt or angry. I tried using the silent treatment at times but that did not work for me. My husband would also retaliate with yelling or staying quiet. The bottom line was that none of the issues that were bothering both of us were ever resolved. You both must directly address the issue with openness and honesty. Just talk to one another with respect.

Please do not withhold your affections from each other after resolving a conflict. The Bible commands that we forgive. One did not lose to the other. Rather, both of you won. Forgiveness always opens the door to becoming more close. Such closeness creates an atmosphere of love and that will lead to genuine intimacy. I exhort you to be intimate because there is powerful healing unleashed in this form of communication. The act of intimacy breaks any power the enemy has over your anger. Your physical union in the natural exemplifies the spiritual union of your hearts and spirits. Such intimacy serves only to strengthen your marriage.

It is mission critical to spend ample quality time together as husbands and wives. There is barely enough time to spare for ourselves in today's busy world. How much less then for our spouses and/or children? It is no real wonder why our marriage starts falling apart. I once read a quote from Mary Kay Ash (the founder of Mary Kay Cosmetics) who said, "It is imperative to put God first, family second, and career third." This is so crucial. The world today seems to have it backwards. Rekindle your romance. Always remember your courtship and honeymoon. Never forget the core reason why you chose this special person to be your lifetime partner out from millions of others.

It is just as important to spend time with your spouse as it is your children. Think about it. If your marriage fails then your children will suffer. So make time for your spouse and have a regular date night. If finances are tight then take a walk in the park or the mall. I know some couples that revolve everything around their children. Is the marriage union between you and your spouse or between you and your children? What happens to the marriage once the children are grown and gone? This is why it is so important to set some standards.

You have a list of activities that interest each of you. Some might be mutual and others may not. Wives, try and engage in some of the healthy activities that interest your husbands. Husbands should do the same. Sharing activities as a couple brings about bonding and togetherness. This is a tried and true way to prevent temptations from creeping into your marriage.

Please do not neglect your bodily appearance or health, either. If your husband likes for you to look good for him then do it. You will actually make yourself feel better in the process. The same goes for your spouse. There is something to be said about how one feels and perceives themselves after they have dressed-up to their comfort level and receive compliments in return. It makes you feel good when you get noticed for all the right reasons. Your whole demeanor and attitude shifts in a positive way. You actually make the world a better place when you are feeling good about yourself. Everybody likes to be validated. Do not let a slight weight gain or superficial imperfections hinder you.

Money causes a lot of marriage problems. It doesn't really matter who makes the most money in the marriage if you are both in one accord. Many women today have higher incomes than men. Sometimes there is a positional shift in a marriage because of unequal income levels. It is a fact that men have egos and they like to feel like the head of the house even if the woman makes more money or all the money. Do not allow the power you have in making the most money to distract you of your role in the marriage. Life has many surprises. One day you may not be the one bringing in the most money due to any number of circumstances that can occur in life. So I highly recommend that you honor what is said in the Bible:

In Ephesians 5:22-33, "Wives, submit to your husbands as to the Lord. For the husband is the head of the wife as Christ is the head of the church, His body, of which He is the Savior. Now as the church submits to Christ, so also wives should submit to their husbands in everything. Husbands, love your wives just as Christ loved the church and gave Himself up for her to make her holy, cleansing her by the washing with water through the Word, and to present her to Himself as a radiant church, without stain or wrinkle or any other blemish, but holy and blameless. In this same way, husbands ought to love their wives as their own bodies. He who loves his wife loves himself. After all, no one ever hated his own body, but feeds and cares for it, just as Christ does the church, for we are members of His body. For this reason a man will leave his father and mother and be united to his wife, and the two will become one flesh. This is a profound mystery, but I am talking about Christ and the church. However, each one of you also must love his wife as he loves himself, and the wife must respect her husband."

Husband, if you love your wife as you love the Lord and yourself then you can overcome anything that occurs in marriage. If your wife is a stay at home mom, has a job, or makes more money than you then encourage her and validate the work she is doing with positive reinforcement. Wives, this also applies to you.

We are quick to point out each other's faults. How about expressing your gratitude and appreciation for the positive things that you do for each other? It is very important, try this and reap its effects.

Temptations commonly occur in marriage. A temptation is not a sin until you yield to it. Some married couples battle the temptation of adultery, some alcoholism, gambling, substance abuse, verbal, physical, emotional and mental abuse. If these issues arise in your marriage then how would you cope with it? I've found out that it takes both knowing God _and_ knowing the Word of God in order to make the best choices in one's life that will make a marriage work. Both partners will need to be in agreement to seek help from a qualified spiritual marriage leader who can counsel them on the teachings of marital principles from the Word of God!

If you aren't married yet then pray for God's best and His perfect will to be done about you finding your life partner or "soul mate". Wait for God to reveal that person to you. If you meet someone then commit the relationship to God's hands. Ask Him for His perfect will before you get involved emotionally or physically. Be patient and wait. The Lord always honors obedience and will reveal to you if that person is your life partner or not. Be sure and praise Him for His faithfulness whether the revelation was what you expected or not. He alone knows what is best for you. Once His perfect will is done concerning who to marry, you will still face certain challenges in the marriage. If you have been learning anything at all from this book then you will know to give it all to Him. Don't let a ticking biological clock or any other factors cause you to rush into a commitment that is not God's best. Just be patient. Wait on God! His best is always a blessing worth waiting for.

Chapter Ten

WHAT IS YOUR STORY?

"And if anyone is a worshiper of God and does His will, He hears Him."

(John 9:31)

What is your Story?

Everyone has a story. If you are reading this book then perhaps you have something that you have done or someone has done to you that you are not proud of. You cannot forgive yourself and you cannot let it go. Whatever occurred is hindering your progress in your walk with God.

"Then said Jesus, Father, forgive them; for they know not what they do. And they parted his raiment, and cast lots." *(Luke 23:34)*

Your story might be the same or totally different from mine. Whatever your story is, God wants you to know it does not matter as long as you have repented in your heart and asked for His forgiveness, He has forgiven you. The question then becomes, "Have you forgiven yourself?"

"Brothers, I do not consider myself yet to have taken hold of it. But one thing I do: forgetting what is behind and straining toward what is ahead, I press on toward the goal to win the prize for which God has called me heavenward in Christ Jesus." (Philippians 3:13, 14)

Remember all sin is equal in the eyes of the Holy God. Therefore, the sin of the person who told the little white lie is no different from the person who committed adultery or murder. It is only by His grace that we are saved and forgiven. Become knowledgeable in the Lord and know your place with the Lord. Why be confused about God when you can know Him? Know that by His Son's death and resurrection that you have been made righteous with God. Do not take on the fight by yourself. Allow Him to fight for you. Talk to Him in prayer. Release all your burdens on Him. If you could do it by yourself then your life would be perfect and without sin. But we cannot do it all by ourselves. It is not by our strength or might but by His Spirit of grace and mercy says the Lord. Allow Him to take over. Yield control to Him and see a miraculous difference in all aspects of your life.

How do you forgive those that have hurt you?

"For if you forgive men when they sin against you; your heavenly Father will also forgive you. But if you do not forgive men their sins, your Father will not forgive your sins." (Matthew 6:14, 15)

With Christ, all things are possible. You can forgive those who have hurt you by relying on Jesus Christ and allowing Him to do His work in you. It is nearly impossible to forgive those who have hurt you or caused you affliction without God's grace.

I recently lost my father to cancer. An injustice was done to me by a close family member as I was in the midst of making arrangements for his funeral. I was very hurt and upset when I found out. I was so angry that I almost fell into sin. My husband Osei suggested that we just stay home from church. I was exhausted so I agreed. We were invited to a christening that same afternoon and I did not feel like going to that either. As I lay in bed, I felt a nudging to go with my family to the christening at our family member's church later on that morning. I shared this with my husband. He said we should obey and go. So we left the house right away because it was late. I was so afraid we had missed it. To my delight, the christening ceremony was just about to begin. It was so beautiful. Then the preaching began.

The sermon was delivered by Pastor Kwame Frimpong who was visiting. The message was on "forgiveness" and it was so powerful that everyone in the sanctuary was visibly touched. After the service, I spoke to Pastor Kwame about God's plan for me to write a book on forgiveness but I was stuck. Pastor Kwame said that he had authored several books and was more than willing to help me with my first book. His gift is helping people find their God ordained purpose. We felt connected right away and decided to set a time when our families could meet informally. Now the rest is history. With that encouragement, I was able to write the book in a few weeks to everyone's surprise. Isn't God amazing? Here was a situation where the enemy was trying to keep me from attending church and if I had not gone then I would have completely missed my divine appointment that would have led to finishing my book! That is the mighty power of God!

Pastor Kwame's preaching touched me very much. The Holy Spirit convicted me. The next day I picked up the phone, called my family member who had done the injustice to me and made peace with him in a godly way. It felt good and right.

Chapter Eleven

OUR WAYS ARE NOT GOD'S WAYS

"The things which are impossible with men are possible with God."

(Luke 18:27)

Have you ever wondered why you continue to pray even when you feel like God isn't answering them? Do you question the reason for tragic and unfortunate events that happen to you or your friends? We may not always understand why God permits these kinds of things to occur. These painful and disturbing situations serve to illustrate that our ways definitely are not God's ways.

One thing is certain. God is the all inclusive and omnipotent Creator who knew us before we were even conceived. He knows our past, present and future. He knows of the happiness as well as the heartaches we will endure in our lifetime. He gives us a free will then watches how we conduct our lives. Will we give it all back to Him? Isn't He an able God who knows our innermost desires and hurts? Never forget that it is during our darkest moments in life that He carries us.

I can't explain to you why He allows certain situations to happen. But I can assure you that He knows why they should happen. He never promised that there would not be heartache in the world. He never promised that we are exempt from various trials and tribulations during life. What He has promised is in the midst of all the chaos and hurts that He will handle it for us. If we give it all to Him then He will lead us to the path of righteousness. We should be able to completely trust Him because we know that He is a God who never deviates from His promises. So why don't we just trust in Him and lay it all at His feet? Could it be unbelief?

Can you imagine going through grief without allowing God in? The grieving process after losing a close relative is one of the most painful and deepest sorrows there is in life. It is never easy to lose a loved one. Even more difficult would be the sudden death of a child.

In moments like these we should just give it all to God. He knows what is best. We can confidently allow Him to mend our hearts and trust in His ways. We certainly would not allow our loved ones to die if we could prevent it. All of us would choose peace rather than chaos. The good news is we can if we cast all of our burdens upon Him. But that's easier said than done.

Annie's story

Annie and her husband were blessed with two beautiful daughters. They were a very close knit family. Their love for God and each other was apparent to everyone around them. One day tragedy struck. Annie's older daughter was riding in a car driven by Annie's father. Grandfather and granddaughter never arrived at their destination.

Annie and her husband received the call that every parent dreads. They were informed that a terrible car accident had occurred and they should come right away to the hospital. The loving parents were greeted with the grim news that their daughter did not survive. She had been pronounced dead at the scene of the accident. She was only eleven years old. Annie's father had suffered burns to over seventy percent of his body. The Emergency Room successfully stabilized his condition. Then he was flown to a larger hospital with a burn unit for continuity of care.

The entire family was understandably devastated and lost. They lived in a small town. The details of the accident were reported in the local newspaper the very next day as well as on the local TV news. Many people prayed for them. Only God's grace and healing mercy can ease the pain and sorrow at such a time as this. At first, Annie and her family did not understand why this tragic accident had to happen and especially to them. But our ways are not God's ways. Our wants are not His wants. Annie and her family knew that God was in control. They will never forget their daughter and still miss her terribly. But they have to just lay it all at His feet.

Annie's father went through an extensive recovery stage followed by rehabilitation. He is currently living with Annie and her family in their home.

My prayer is that Annie's father will not blame himself for the tragic car accident which claimed the life of his precious granddaughter. He should rejoice in the fact that he is alive. The Bible clearly states that tomorrow is not promised to any of us. "There is a time to be born and a time to die." For Annie, it was her daughter's time and not her fathers. God's ways are not our ways. We need to develop a grateful heart and rejoice in the fact that He knows better than we do.

Joshua's story

Joshua is a young man who was born healthy and normal. He grew up just like any other three year old boy. Then Joshua started complaining of constant headaches and his eyesight bothered him. He was examined and the diagnosis was that Joshua had a brain tumor. The tumor was removed. A couple of years passed then Joshua had a recurrence of the tumor with several other complications. The treatment wasn't easy but Joshua made it. His dedicated grandmother became his primary care taker and gave him excellent care.

Joshua was left with many challenges after his ordeal ended. He lost eyesight in his left eye. His growth was stunted. He could not breathe on his own for long periods of time because some of his lung was removed. The doctors performed a tracheotomy and Joshua was placed on a mechanical ventilator (a breathing machine). *Tracheotomy is a surgically created opening in the neck which leads directly to the trachea (the breathing tube). It is kept open with a hollow tube called a tracheotomy tube.*

He could not eat nor swallow on his own without aspirating (choking) so he had to get a PEG tube to help him eat. *(Percutaneous Endoscopic Gastrostomy i.e. PEG tube) is a feeding tube. It is a medical procedure where a tube is passed into a patient's stomach via the abdomen to provide a means of feeding when oral intake is not adequate or possible.*

Joshua lost his speech and is unable to speak. But he understands everything going on around him. He uses hand motions to effectively communicate his wants and needs from his wheel chair.

Joshua has had many other challenges in his young life. He's been resuscitated (being brought back to life) after his heart stopped several times. He is now in his early twenties but has the mental development of an eight year old. He continues to face many medical challenges. God knows why Joshua is alive. He touches all those that are blessed to meet and know him.

I am proud to say that I am one of those privileged individuals. Joshua is an inspiration to me. I truly understand appreciating life and its blessings. We really should stop complaining of all we do not have and be thankful for all that we do have.

Throughout Joshua's ordeal, he is still a happy person. He is content with his life and believes that there is a reason for his existence. He is blessed to be alive despite all that he has to endure. His grandmother is Joshua's biggest cheerleader. She is also one of the most attentive and caring caregivers that I have ever encountered. Being in their company is a sheer delight that approaches experiencing the true mystery and miracle of God.

May God continue to bless Joshua, his grandmother and all that is committed to them. May God use his life story and experiences to be an inspiration to all that meet him and read about him. God's ways are not our ways. God bless you Joshua and Ms. Rebecca (Joshua's grandmother and caretaker).

Chapter Twelve

THE BENEFITS OF FORGIVENESS

Proverbs 17:9 tells us that, *"a real friend will forgive."*

The benefits of forgiving

If you are like me, you have been hurt by someone at one point or another. Life includes the pain of being sinned against. There are some hurts that are difficult to forgive and forget. Sometimes these hurts or injustices leave a lasting impression on you. They can bring about feelings of anger, rejection, and bitterness that are difficult to overcome. If you do not practice forgiveness then the negative feelings associated with an injustice will tear you down. No one likes to be wrongly accused, mistreated, abused, lied to, or hurt, but these things are a fact of life and eventually they happen to each of us.

Learning how to forgive is just plain good for you. There are proven spiritual, mental, emotional and physical benefits. For instance, when you forgive, you will experience less stress, depression, anxiety, hostility, pain, and even decreased risk of alcohol or substance abuse. If you let go of offenses then you can experience extraordinary compassion and peace which will ultimately lead to your spiritual and psychological well being.

I know people who have held on to injustices for so long that it dictates their life. Some have turned to drugs, alcohol, stealing, murder, promiscuity, abusive relationships, being the abuser and much more. I am sure you know some of these people as well. Who are they hurting? They aren't hurting the one who did them the injustice. No, they are only hurting themselves and blocking off their chance at happiness and many other blessings waiting for them to claim. If they actually examine their situation carefully and give it all to God, they will realize that all the pain and anguish that they are going through (which will subsequently affect their loved ones) can be avoided.

Forgiveness is both a state of the mind and a way of life. It is a choice which requires a conscious action on your part. Remember that forgiveness is not a gift to your offender but a gift to you. Allow yourself to see the benefits of forgiving others and how that will affect your life. Meditate for a moment on the physical and spiritual aspect forgiveness will have on your well being.

Consider how forgiving others can help you overcome the power the offense has over you. If you need to then you should pray for God to help you be a forgiver. We are all called to follow Jesus' example on the cross when he prayed, "Father forgive them for they know not what they do." When you forgive and let it go, you are no longer a victim but a conqueror.

You have overcome and are the winner. It doesn't matter if your offender has apologized or not. Let it go and give it all to God. Allow Him to mend and heal your heart.

Do you realize that often we wait for our offender to feel bad about what they have done and apologize? Sometimes they will and sometimes they won't. If they fail to apologize then don't allow their lack of accountability, conviction and repentance to control your emotions and negatively affect your destiny. Decide to forgive others who have caused you affliction and start healing. This is obedience to the command "Forgive others as you have been forgiven".

It takes a very special person to exercise forgiveness in the face of a devastating loss or event. During times of hardship we should look to God as our source for the inner strength and peace that we need to keep going. Some sins are nearly impossible to forgive without God's help. It is particularly difficult to forgive your partner after they have had an affair. What remains is deep emotional pain, distrust and low self esteem.

Infidelity does not have to be the end of your marriage. With God's help and through prayer, you can mend your relationship if you both have the same commitment for rebuilding the marriage. God hates divorce but allows it in cases of adultery. Just because God allows something doesn't mean that it is His perfect will. If you pray, seek support from a spiritual leader or counselor and give yourself time to heal then restoration can happen. In many cases the marriage becomes much stronger than it was previously. Forgiveness does not mean that the offense is justified or acceptable. Rather, it is a conscious state of mind to let go of an offense or event before holding you in bondage.

Harvard Women's Health Watch discusses the following five positive health effects of forgiving that have been scientifically studied:

Forgiveness:

Reduce stress: Researchers found that mentally nursing a grudge puts your body through the same strains as a major stressful event: Muscles tense, blood pressure rises, and sweating increases.

Promotes better heart health: One study found a link between forgiving someone for a betrayal and improvements in blood pressure and heart rate, and a decreased workload for the heart.

Establish stronger relationships: A 2004 study showed that women who were able to forgive their spouses and feel benevolent toward them resolved conflicts more effectively.

Reduce pain: A small study on people with chronic back pain found that those who practiced meditation focusing on converting anger to compassion felt less pain and anxiety than those who received regular care.

Promote greater happiness: When you forgive someone, you make yourself rather than the person who hurt you responsible for your happiness. One survey showed that people who talk about forgiveness during psychotherapy sessions experience greater improvements than those who don't.

Harvard Health Publications, *"Power of Forgiveness – Forgive Others"*, December 2004

The Bible says in Matthew 6:12; forgive us our debts, as we also have forgiven our debtors. It goes on to say in Matthew 6:14-15; "for if you forgive men when they sin against you, your heavenly Father will also forgive you. But if you do not forgive men their sins, your Father will not forgive your sins."

So my friend, take control and do not give dominion to the enemy over your joy, life and blessings that are waiting for you. Forgiveness is a choice and a good choice that brings many benefits. Remember, forgiveness is a gift to yourself and for God to be glorified. Never forget how it felt to be forgiven when you offended someone. If you sin and ask God for forgiveness then you want to be forgiven, right? So work hard with God's help at granting forgiveness. As a result you will reap the spiritual, mental and physical benefits that come from forgiving others.

Chapter Thirteen, Conclusion

FORGIVENESS IS A GIFT FOR US ALL

In Colossians 3, the Bible tells us the rules of Holy Living. In particular, *Colossians 3:13,* it tells us to, *"Bear with each other and forgive whatever grievances you may have against one other. Forgive as the Lord forgave you. And over all these virtues put love, which binds them all together in perfect unity."*

I was at a loss for words and understanding when God laid it on my heart to write this book. So I asked God to show me how and to give me the wisdom in order to share with you all what He wanted us to learn. I inquired of Him further about why He wanted me to write about forgiveness when there were already many books on the topic. He laid on my heart to simply write and gave assurance that the Holy Spirit would guide me. He promised to provide the resources and people that I would need to help me write this book. He assured me that He will bring about what He wants to share with His children.

I was able to let go of many injustices and offenses done to me by writing this book. Not in my wildest dreams did I know that I was going to be the one who was going to receive the biggest healing and blessing! I have been able to forgive others through God's mercy, prayers and allowing Him to heal me. I've also prayed for God to heal and mend the broken hearts of those whom I have hurt and ask for their forgiveness. It has been humbling and powerful, bringing forth a total transformation in my life. This entire process and experience has elevated my faith and walk with our Living God whom we serve. I feel liberated, light, and free in my spirit. I pray that He will continue to use me for His perfect will.

My friend, I am not unique in what He has called me to do. We all have been bestowed and blessed with gifts. There is a higher calling and purpose for each of our lives. It is a matter of seeking and asking Him to manifest His perfect will in your life. Believe that God is able to do an abundance of all things. His ways are not our ways, but His way is far superior to ours.

Therefore, do not block your blessings by allowing past hurts and injustices to control your life and destiny. Don't allow the enemy access. He would love to have power and dominion over your past or present hurts so that you can do sometimes what is called the "unthinkable".

When you get hurt, (*and as long as we have the breath of life in us we will experience hurt in one form or another*) pray and ask God for the healing power to forgive and be free. The healing in forgiveness is not for the people who caused the pain or hurt but it is for you. It is for you to be free and liberated in order to properly serve God and to receive the blessings that He has for you. Therefore, in forgiving others who have hurt us, we are giving ourselves a gift in order to gain a stronger spiritual, psychological, mental and physical well being.

In these days of economic crisis, war, natural disasters and governmental meltdowns, who can we look to, but to God our Father for peace and serenity? We may not always understand or get all the answers to our questions, but He understands and knows why. He knew all of these things would happen before they occurred. Only in Him can we dwell and say, "may Your will be done." Only in Him is perfect peace and calmness. If you still doubt then test yourself by immersing yourself totally in Him. Why does it feel so good and peaceful? Is that feeling of love, humbleness and peace that you're feeling coming from a bad place? I do not think so! Just believe that we serve a living God. Do not doubt. Give it all to Him.

Sinning is human nature. We all fall short of God's glory and it is only by His grace that we are saved. We can't save ourselves. Salvation is for us all but only by believing in His son Jesus Christ and in His life, death and resurrection can we be made whole again. Therefore, when we sin we need to pray and confess our sins, ask for forgiveness and repent. We should believe that as we pray, our sins are forgiven and we in turn need to forgive ourselves and others. My prayer is that whatever you experience throughout life, whether good or bad, that you lay it at God's feet and trust in Him because He is able. In doing this, be ready and watch the miracles flow in your life. May God continue to be with you and bless you!

If you have not received salvation and you are ready to accept the Lord Jesus Christ as your personal Savior then say this prayer:

Dear God,

I don't know You and I do not have a relationship with You. I have come because I am ready to know You and want to have a personal relationship with You. I am ready to be made righteous in You by accepting Your son Jesus Christ as my personal Savior. I believe that only by His life, death and resurrection will I be born again. I have tried it on my own and I have not succeeded. I am hurting and I am lost but I now know the only way to salvation is accepting You and allowing You to make changes in my life. It is only by Your grace and mercy, not by my might or strength. I am ready Lord. Thank you for accepting me and lead me to the path of righteousness.

Amen!

If you have received salvation, but have fallen along the way and want a stronger relationship with Jesus Christ, then pray this:

Dear God,

I want to have a stronger relationship with You. I have been doing it on my own. Now I see such a difference from when I allowed You to lead me. I am sorry for all that I have done that fell short of Your glory. I recommit myself to You and Jesus Christ. I ask for You to lead me again to the path of righteousness. I confess and repent of my sins. Thank you for forgiving me and receiving me. Help me to lead a life that is exemplary to You, so that I can win souls for You. Have Your way with me and may all the glory go to You. Thank you!

Amen!

In *Psalm 103:11* we see the magnitude of God's love for us. For the bible says, *"for as high as the heavens are above the earth, so great is his love for those who fear him."*

BE BLESSED!

About The Author

D r. Jacqueline Owusu (Dr. Jackie) is a Christian motivational speaker, physician, author, wife and mother of two boys. She is actively pursuing her call to motivate and encourage others to live a burden free life by knowing their place with God. The solution is overcoming life's trials and tribulations by receiving salvation in Jesus Christ and allowing the Holy Spirit to reveal the living Word of God. Only then will each person be directed to the path of righteousness and the unique destiny God has for their life. Her goal is to encourage people to see who they are in Christ no matter what circumstances surround them.

Dr. Jackie was born in Ghana, West Africa and came to the United States in 1981 to rejoin her family. She felt a deep seated need for love and affection after being separated as an infant until she was ten years old. Looking for the answer to this need took her into "all the wrong places" while growing up into adulthood. Dr. Jackie was finally liberated when she received salvation and developed a close personal relationship with Jesus Christ. She is so full of joy and hope that her new mission in life is helping others experience this same freedom by overcoming whatever is holding them back from receiving their blessings.

After high school, Dr. Jackie received an undergraduate degree in Biochemistry, and a Masters Degree in Public Administration (MPA). Then after attending medical school she was awarded a Doctor of Medicine degree (MD), specializing and becoming Board Certified in Internal Medicine.

As a practicing physician and grateful to God for allowing her to serve in this capacity, she still felt a void in her life. There was no sense of contentment with her life. The question, "Besides being a doctor and owning several businesses, is that all there is to my life?" gnawed at her. So she started searching for what the "missing" more could be.

That search for significance led Dr. Jackie again to God for the answers. One day, she felt a nudging "to let go and let God." She broke down and cried out, "Father God, I want Your perfect will and purpose to be done in my life." By His Grace, Dr. Jackie's life began to change.

She had known for a very long time that there was a calling of ministry on her life but she had been running away from it. She always says, "You can run only for so long from God but at His appointed time, you can no longer run."

Now, bolstered by the knowledge that she has obtained through her life experiences, Dr. Jackie is sure "without a doubt" that she is being obedient to her ministry calling to motivate and encourage others to live free in God. She also uses her gift of singing to minister songs that will help heal the wounded soul. Her favorite saying is, "It is better to look at the glass as half full instead of half empty when God is your Father!" By letting God, He will ultimately allow you to become the best YOU that you can be!

Dr. Jackie has been married to her husband Nana Osei Bediako for over ten years. They have two sons, Matthew and Michael. Nana Osei, Dr. Jackie and their children live near Atlanta, Georgia. They attend church at River of Life Chapel under the presiding pastor Bishop Joe Kwapong.

CPSIA information can be obtained at www.ICGtesting.com
Printed in the USA
LVOW12s2005150614

390138LV00024B/1196/P